50 Premium American Bread Dishes in the Oven

By: Kelly Johnson

Table of Contents

- Classic American Cornbread
- Soft Dinner Rolls
- Buttermilk Biscuits
- Banana Bread
- Pumpkin Bread
- Cinnamon Swirl Bread
- Focaccia with Rosemary
- Brioche Bread
- Sourdough Bread
- Jalapeño Cheddar Bread
- Potato Bread
- Honey Wheat Bread
- Garlic Herb Bread
- Apple Cinnamon Bread
- Zucchini Bread
- Oatmeal Bread
- French Toast Casserole
- Challah Bread
- Cranberry Orange Bread
- Whole Wheat Sandwich Bread
- Rye Bread
- Pumpernickel Bread
- Beer Bread
- Maple Walnut Bread
- Milk Bread
- Cheese Stuffed Bread
- Olive Oil and Sea Salt Focaccia
- Bacon Cheddar Bread
- Sweet Potato Bread
- Apple and Walnut Bread
- Hot Cross Buns
- Stuffed Garlic Bread
- Tomato Basil Bread
- Blueberry Lemon Bread
- Spicy Cheddar Cornbread

- Chocolate Chip Banana Bread
- Cinnamon Rolls
- Peach and Almond Bread
- Pecan Bread
- Cranberry Almond Bread
- Herb and Parmesan Breadsticks
- Asiago Cheese Bread
- Pretzel Bread
- Coconut Bread
- Maple Pecan Bread
- Lemon Poppy Seed Bread
- Fig and Walnut Bread
- Sweet Cornbread with Jalapeños
- Carrot Raisin Bread
- Bacon and Chive Bread

Classic American Cornbread

Ingredients:

- 1 cup cornmeal
- 1 cup all-purpose flour
- 1/4 cup sugar
- 1 tbsp baking powder
- 1/2 tsp salt
- 1 cup buttermilk
- 2 large eggs
- 1/4 cup unsalted butter, melted

Instructions:

1. Preheat the oven to 425°F (220°C). Grease or line an 8x8-inch baking pan.
2. In a large bowl, whisk together the cornmeal, flour, sugar, baking powder, and salt.
3. In a separate bowl, whisk together the buttermilk, eggs, and melted butter.
4. Pour the wet ingredients into the dry ingredients and stir until just combined.
5. Pour the batter into the prepared pan and spread it out evenly.
6. Bake for 20-25 minutes, or until a toothpick inserted into the center comes out clean. Serve warm.

Soft Dinner Rolls

Ingredients:

- 3 1/2 cups all-purpose flour
- 1 packet (2 1/4 tsp) active dry yeast
- 1/4 cup sugar
- 1 tsp salt
- 1 cup warm milk
- 1/4 cup unsalted butter, melted
- 1 large egg

Instructions:

1. In a bowl, combine warm milk, sugar, and yeast. Let it sit for about 5 minutes until it becomes foamy.
2. In a large mixing bowl, whisk together the flour and salt. Add the yeast mixture, melted butter, and egg. Mix until a dough forms.
3. Knead the dough on a floured surface for about 5-7 minutes, or until smooth and elastic.
4. Place the dough in a greased bowl, cover with a clean towel, and let it rise for 1-1.5 hours, or until doubled in size.
5. Preheat the oven to 375°F (190°C). Punch down the dough and divide it into 12 equal pieces.
6. Shape the dough into rolls and place them in a greased 9x13-inch baking pan.
7. Cover and let the rolls rise for 30 minutes. Bake for 18-20 minutes, or until golden brown. Brush with melted butter before serving.

Buttermilk Biscuits

Ingredients:

- 2 cups all-purpose flour
- 1 tbsp baking powder
- 1/2 tsp salt
- 1/2 tsp baking soda
- 1/2 cup cold unsalted butter, cubed
- 3/4 cup buttermilk

Instructions:

1. Preheat the oven to 450°F (230°C). Grease a baking sheet or line it with parchment paper.
2. In a large bowl, whisk together the flour, baking powder, salt, and baking soda.
3. Cut in the cold butter using a pastry cutter or your fingers until the mixture resembles coarse crumbs.
4. Add the buttermilk and stir gently until the dough just comes together.
5. Turn the dough onto a floured surface and gently fold it over a few times. Pat it down to about 1-inch thickness.
6. Use a biscuit cutter to cut out biscuits and place them on the prepared baking sheet.
7. Bake for 10-12 minutes, or until golden brown. Serve warm.

Banana Bread

Ingredients:

- 2-3 ripe bananas, mashed
- 1/2 cup unsalted butter, melted
- 1 cup sugar
- 2 large eggs
- 1 tsp vanilla extract
- 1 1/2 cups all-purpose flour
- 1 tsp baking soda
- 1/2 tsp salt

Instructions:

1. Preheat the oven to 350°F (175°C). Grease a 9x5-inch loaf pan.
2. In a large bowl, mix the mashed bananas, melted butter, sugar, eggs, and vanilla extract.
3. In a separate bowl, whisk together the flour, baking soda, and salt.
4. Add the dry ingredients to the wet ingredients and stir until just combined.
5. Pour the batter into the prepared loaf pan and smooth the top.
6. Bake for 60-65 minutes, or until a toothpick inserted into the center comes out clean. Let cool before slicing.

Pumpkin Bread

Ingredients:

- 1 3/4 cups all-purpose flour
- 1 1/2 tsp baking soda
- 1/2 tsp salt
- 1 tsp cinnamon
- 1/2 tsp nutmeg
- 1/2 tsp cloves
- 1 cup sugar
- 1/2 cup vegetable oil
- 2 large eggs
- 1 1/2 cups canned pumpkin
- 1/4 cup water
- 1 tsp vanilla extract

Instructions:

1. Preheat the oven to 350°F (175°C). Grease a 9x5-inch loaf pan.
2. In a medium bowl, whisk together the flour, baking soda, salt, and spices.
3. In a large bowl, beat together the sugar, oil, eggs, pumpkin, water, and vanilla.
4. Add the dry ingredients to the wet ingredients and stir until just combined.
5. Pour the batter into the prepared loaf pan and smooth the top.
6. Bake for 60-65 minutes, or until a toothpick comes out clean. Let cool before serving.

Cinnamon Swirl Bread

Ingredients:

- 2 cups all-purpose flour
- 1/4 cup sugar
- 2 1/4 tsp active dry yeast
- 1 tsp salt
- 3/4 cup warm milk
- 2 tbsp unsalted butter, melted
- 1 egg
- 1 tbsp ground cinnamon
- 1/4 cup brown sugar

Instructions:

1. In a large bowl, combine flour, sugar, yeast, and salt. Add warm milk, melted butter, and egg. Mix to form a dough.
2. Knead the dough on a floured surface for 5-7 minutes until smooth. Place in a greased bowl, cover, and let rise for 1 hour.
3. Preheat the oven to 350°F (175°C). Punch down the dough and roll it out into a rectangle.
4. Mix cinnamon and brown sugar, then sprinkle it evenly over the dough.
5. Roll the dough up into a log and place it in a greased loaf pan.
6. Let the dough rise for 30 minutes, then bake for 25-30 minutes, or until golden brown.

Focaccia with Rosemary

Ingredients:

- 3 cups all-purpose flour
- 2 1/4 tsp active dry yeast
- 1 tbsp sugar
- 1 tsp salt
- 1/4 cup olive oil
- 1 cup warm water
- 1 tbsp fresh rosemary, chopped

Instructions:

1. In a bowl, mix the yeast, sugar, and warm water. Let sit for 5 minutes until foamy.
2. Add the flour, salt, and olive oil to the yeast mixture. Stir to form a dough.
3. Knead the dough on a floured surface for 5-7 minutes. Place it in an oiled bowl, cover, and let rise for 1 hour.
4. Preheat the oven to 400°F (200°C). Punch down the dough and press it into an oiled baking sheet.
5. Sprinkle with rosemary and a drizzle of olive oil. Bake for 20-25 minutes, until golden brown.

Brioche Bread

Ingredients:

- 3 1/4 cups all-purpose flour
- 1/4 cup sugar
- 2 tsp active dry yeast
- 1 tsp salt
- 5 large eggs
- 1 cup unsalted butter, cubed and softened
- 1/4 cup warm milk

Instructions:

1. In a large bowl, mix the yeast, sugar, and warm milk. Let sit for 5 minutes until foamy.
2. Add the flour and salt, then beat in the eggs one at a time.
3. Add the butter, a few cubes at a time, and knead until smooth, about 10 minutes.
4. Let the dough rise in an oiled bowl, covered, for 2 hours.
5. Preheat the oven to 375°F (190°C). Shape the dough into a loaf and place it in a greased pan.
6. Bake for 30-35 minutes, until golden brown. Let cool before slicing.

Sourdough Bread

Ingredients:

- 1 cup sourdough starter
- 3 cups all-purpose flour
- 1 1/2 tsp salt
- 1 cup warm water

Instructions:

1. In a large bowl, combine the sourdough starter, flour, and salt.
2. Add warm water and stir until the dough forms.
3. Knead for 5-7 minutes on a floured surface.
4. Let the dough rise in a bowl, covered, for 4 hours.
5. Preheat the oven to 450°F (230°C). Punch down the dough and shape it into a round loaf.
6. Bake for 30-35 minutes, until golden brown. Let cool before slicing.

Jalapeño Cheddar Bread

Ingredients:

- 2 cups all-purpose flour
- 1 cup shredded cheddar cheese
- 1-2 jalapeños, finely chopped (seeds removed for less heat)
- 1 tbsp baking powder
- 1/2 tsp salt
- 1/2 tsp garlic powder
- 1/2 cup milk
- 1/4 cup unsalted butter, melted
- 2 large eggs

Instructions:

1. Preheat the oven to 375°F (190°C). Grease or line a loaf pan.
2. In a large bowl, combine flour, cheddar cheese, jalapeños, baking powder, salt, and garlic powder.
3. In a separate bowl, whisk together milk, melted butter, and eggs.
4. Add the wet ingredients to the dry ingredients and stir until just combined.
5. Pour the batter into the prepared loaf pan and smooth the top.
6. Bake for 40-45 minutes, or until golden brown and a toothpick comes out clean. Let cool before slicing.

Potato Bread

Ingredients:

- 2 cups mashed potatoes (about 2 medium potatoes)
- 1/2 cup warm milk
- 1/4 cup unsalted butter, melted
- 1 tbsp sugar
- 1 tsp salt
- 2 1/4 tsp active dry yeast
- 4 cups all-purpose flour

Instructions:

1. Preheat the oven to 375°F (190°C). Grease a 9x5-inch loaf pan.
2. In a small bowl, combine warm milk, sugar, and yeast. Let sit for about 5 minutes until foamy.
3. In a large mixing bowl, combine mashed potatoes, melted butter, and salt. Add the yeast mixture and stir to combine.
4. Gradually add flour, one cup at a time, until a soft dough forms.
5. Knead the dough on a floured surface for 5-7 minutes, until smooth.
6. Place the dough in a greased bowl, cover, and let rise for 1-1.5 hours, or until doubled in size.
7. Punch down the dough and shape it into a loaf. Place it in the prepared pan and let rise for another 30 minutes.
8. Bake for 30-35 minutes, or until golden brown. Cool before slicing.

Honey Wheat Bread

Ingredients:

- 2 cups whole wheat flour
- 1 cup all-purpose flour
- 1 tbsp sugar
- 1 1/2 tsp salt
- 2 1/4 tsp active dry yeast
- 3/4 cup warm water
- 1/4 cup honey
- 1 tbsp olive oil

Instructions:

1. In a small bowl, dissolve sugar and yeast in warm water. Let sit for 5 minutes.
2. In a large bowl, combine whole wheat flour, all-purpose flour, and salt. Add the yeast mixture, honey, and olive oil.
3. Mix to form a dough, then knead for 5-7 minutes until smooth.
4. Cover the dough and let it rise for 1 hour, or until doubled in size.
5. Preheat the oven to 375°F (190°C). Punch down the dough and shape it into a loaf.
6. Place the dough in a greased loaf pan and let it rise for another 30 minutes.
7. Bake for 25-30 minutes, until golden brown. Let cool before slicing.

Garlic Herb Bread

Ingredients:

- 3 cups all-purpose flour
- 2 tsp active dry yeast
- 1 tsp salt
- 1 tsp sugar
- 1 cup warm water
- 1/4 cup unsalted butter, melted
- 3 cloves garlic, minced
- 1 tbsp fresh rosemary, chopped
- 1 tbsp fresh thyme, chopped

Instructions:

1. In a small bowl, dissolve sugar and yeast in warm water. Let sit for 5 minutes.
2. In a large bowl, combine flour and salt. Add the yeast mixture, melted butter, garlic, rosemary, and thyme. Mix to form a dough.
3. Knead the dough for 5-7 minutes until smooth. Cover and let rise for 1 hour.
4. Preheat the oven to 375°F (190°C). Punch down the dough and shape it into a loaf.
5. Place the dough on a greased baking sheet and let it rise for another 30 minutes.
6. Bake for 25-30 minutes, or until golden brown. Brush with extra melted butter before serving.

Apple Cinnamon Bread

Ingredients:

- 2 cups all-purpose flour
- 1 tsp baking powder
- 1/2 tsp salt
- 1 tsp cinnamon
- 1/2 tsp nutmeg
- 1/2 cup unsalted butter, softened
- 1 cup sugar
- 2 large eggs
- 1 1/2 cups peeled and diced apples (about 1 medium apple)
- 1/2 cup milk
- 1 tsp vanilla extract

Instructions:

1. Preheat the oven to 350°F (175°C). Grease a 9x5-inch loaf pan.
2. In a medium bowl, whisk together flour, baking powder, salt, cinnamon, and nutmeg.
3. In a large bowl, beat the butter and sugar until light and fluffy. Add the eggs, one at a time, and beat until combined.
4. Stir in the diced apples, milk, and vanilla extract.
5. Gradually add the dry ingredients to the wet ingredients and stir until just combined.
6. Pour the batter into the prepared loaf pan and smooth the top.
7. Bake for 50-60 minutes, or until golden brown and a toothpick comes out clean. Let cool before slicing.

Zucchini Bread

Ingredients:

- 2 cups all-purpose flour
- 1 tsp baking soda
- 1/2 tsp salt
- 1 tsp cinnamon
- 2 large eggs
- 1 cup vegetable oil
- 1 1/2 cups sugar
- 2 tsp vanilla extract
- 2 cups grated zucchini (about 1 medium zucchini)

Instructions:

1. Preheat the oven to 350°F (175°C). Grease a 9x5-inch loaf pan.
2. In a medium bowl, whisk together flour, baking soda, salt, and cinnamon.
3. In a large bowl, beat the eggs, oil, sugar, and vanilla extract until combined.
4. Stir in the grated zucchini.
5. Gradually add the dry ingredients to the wet ingredients and mix until just combined.
6. Pour the batter into the prepared loaf pan and smooth the top.
7. Bake for 55-60 minutes, or until a toothpick inserted into the center comes out clean. Let cool before slicing.

Oatmeal Bread

Ingredients:

- 1 1/2 cups rolled oats
- 2 cups warm water
- 2 1/4 tsp active dry yeast
- 1/4 cup honey
- 1/4 cup unsalted butter, softened
- 4 cups all-purpose flour
- 1 1/2 tsp salt

Instructions:

1. In a bowl, combine rolled oats and warm water. Let it sit for 5 minutes.
2. In a separate bowl, dissolve yeast and honey in warm water and let sit for 5 minutes.
3. Combine the yeast mixture with the oat mixture. Add butter, flour, and salt, and stir until a dough forms.
4. Knead the dough for 5-7 minutes until smooth. Let it rise for 1 hour, or until doubled in size.
5. Preheat the oven to 375°F (190°C). Punch down the dough and shape it into a loaf.
6. Let the dough rise for another 30 minutes, then bake for 30-35 minutes, until golden brown.

French Toast Casserole

Ingredients:

- 1 loaf of day-old bread, cubed
- 8 large eggs
- 2 cups milk
- 1/4 cup heavy cream
- 1/4 cup sugar
- 1 tbsp vanilla extract
- 1 tsp ground cinnamon
- 1/2 tsp ground nutmeg
- Maple syrup (for serving)

Instructions:

1. Preheat the oven to 350°F (175°C). Grease a 9x13-inch baking dish.
2. Arrange the cubed bread in the baking dish.
3. In a large bowl, whisk together the eggs, milk, heavy cream, sugar, vanilla extract, cinnamon, and nutmeg.
4. Pour the egg mixture over the bread cubes, pressing down gently to soak the bread.
5. Bake for 40-45 minutes, until golden brown and puffed. Serve with maple syrup.

Challah Bread

Ingredients:

- 4 cups all-purpose flour
- 1/4 cup sugar
- 1 tbsp active dry yeast
- 1 tsp salt
- 1 cup warm water
- 2 tbsp olive oil
- 2 large eggs (plus 1 egg for egg wash)

Instructions:

1. In a bowl, dissolve sugar and yeast in warm water. Let sit for 5 minutes.
2. In a large bowl, combine flour and salt. Add the yeast mixture, olive oil, and eggs. Mix to form a dough.
3. Knead the dough for 7-10 minutes until smooth. Let rise for 1-1.5 hours, or until doubled in size.
4. Preheat the oven to 375°F (190°C). Punch down the dough and divide it into three equal portions.
5. Braid the three portions into a loaf and place it on a greased baking sheet.
6. Brush the loaf with a beaten egg and let it rise for another 30 minutes.
7. Bake for 30-35 minutes, until golden brown. Let cool before slicing.

Cranberry Orange Bread

Ingredients:

- 2 cups all-purpose flour
- 1 cup sugar
- 1 tsp baking powder
- 1/2 tsp baking soda
- 1/4 tsp salt
- 1/2 cup unsalted butter, softened
- 2 large eggs
- 1/2 cup orange juice
- Zest of 1 orange
- 1 1/2 cups fresh cranberries, chopped
- 1/2 cup chopped walnuts (optional)

Instructions:

1. Preheat the oven to 350°F (175°C). Grease a 9x5-inch loaf pan.
2. In a large bowl, combine flour, sugar, baking powder, baking soda, and salt.
3. In a separate bowl, whisk together the butter, eggs, orange juice, and orange zest.
4. Fold the wet ingredients into the dry ingredients until just combined. Gently stir in the cranberries and walnuts (if using).
5. Pour the batter into the prepared loaf pan and smooth the top.
6. Bake for 55-60 minutes, or until golden brown and a toothpick comes out clean. Let cool before slicing.

Whole Wheat Sandwich Bread

Ingredients:

- 2 cups whole wheat flour
- 1 cup all-purpose flour
- 1 tbsp sugar
- 1 1/2 tsp salt
- 2 1/4 tsp active dry yeast
- 1 1/2 cups warm water
- 1 tbsp olive oil

Instructions:

1. In a small bowl, dissolve sugar and yeast in warm water. Let sit for 5 minutes until foamy.
2. In a large bowl, combine whole wheat flour, all-purpose flour, and salt.
3. Add the yeast mixture and olive oil to the flour mixture, and stir until combined.
4. Knead the dough for 5-7 minutes until smooth and elastic.
5. Cover the dough and let it rise for 1 hour, or until doubled in size.
6. Preheat the oven to 375°F (190°C). Punch down the dough and shape it into a loaf.
7. Place the dough in a greased 9x5-inch loaf pan and let it rise for another 30 minutes.
8. Bake for 25-30 minutes, or until golden brown. Cool before slicing.

Rye Bread

Ingredients:

- 2 cups rye flour
- 2 cups all-purpose flour
- 2 tbsp caraway seeds (optional)
- 1 tbsp sugar
- 1 1/2 tsp salt
- 2 1/4 tsp active dry yeast
- 1 1/2 cups warm water
- 1 tbsp olive oil

Instructions:

1. In a small bowl, dissolve sugar and yeast in warm water. Let sit for 5 minutes until foamy.
2. In a large bowl, combine rye flour, all-purpose flour, caraway seeds, and salt.
3. Add the yeast mixture and olive oil, and stir to form a dough.
4. Knead the dough for 7-10 minutes, until smooth and elastic.
5. Cover the dough and let it rise for 1-1.5 hours, or until doubled in size.
6. Preheat the oven to 375°F (190°C). Punch down the dough and shape it into a loaf.
7. Place the dough in a greased loaf pan and let it rise for another 30 minutes.
8. Bake for 30-35 minutes, or until golden brown and hollow-sounding when tapped. Let cool before slicing.

Pumpernickel Bread

Ingredients:

- 1 cup rye flour
- 2 cups all-purpose flour
- 2 tbsp cocoa powder
- 1 tbsp instant coffee
- 1 tbsp sugar
- 1 1/2 tsp salt
- 2 1/4 tsp active dry yeast
- 1 1/2 cups warm water
- 2 tbsp vegetable oil

Instructions:

1. In a small bowl, dissolve sugar and yeast in warm water. Let sit for 5 minutes.
2. In a large bowl, combine rye flour, all-purpose flour, cocoa powder, instant coffee, and salt.
3. Add the yeast mixture and vegetable oil, stirring to form a dough.
4. Knead the dough for 7-10 minutes, until smooth. Cover and let rise for 1-1.5 hours.
5. Preheat the oven to 375°F (190°C). Punch down the dough and shape it into a loaf.
6. Place the dough in a greased loaf pan and let it rise for another 30 minutes.
7. Bake for 35-40 minutes, until golden brown. Let cool before slicing.

Beer Bread

Ingredients:

- 3 cups all-purpose flour
- 1/4 cup sugar
- 1 tbsp baking powder
- 1/2 tsp salt
- 1 can (12 oz) beer (any variety)
- 1/4 cup melted butter

Instructions:

1. Preheat the oven to 375°F (190°C). Grease a 9x5-inch loaf pan.
2. In a large bowl, combine flour, sugar, baking powder, and salt.
3. Pour the beer into the dry ingredients and stir until just combined.
4. Pour the batter into the prepared pan and smooth the top.
5. Drizzle melted butter over the top of the batter.
6. Bake for 40-45 minutes, until golden brown. Let cool before slicing.

Maple Walnut Bread

Ingredients:

- 2 cups all-purpose flour
- 1/2 cup whole wheat flour
- 1/2 cup maple syrup
- 1/2 cup milk
- 1/4 cup unsalted butter, melted
- 2 1/4 tsp active dry yeast
- 1/2 tsp salt
- 1/2 cup chopped walnuts

Instructions:

1. In a small bowl, dissolve yeast in warm milk. Let sit for 5 minutes.
2. In a large bowl, combine flours, salt, and walnuts.
3. Add the yeast mixture, maple syrup, and melted butter to the flour mixture. Stir until a dough forms.
4. Knead the dough for 5-7 minutes until smooth. Cover and let rise for 1 hour.
5. Preheat the oven to 375°F (190°C). Punch down the dough and shape it into a loaf.
6. Let the dough rise for another 30 minutes. Bake for 30-35 minutes, or until golden brown. Cool before slicing.

Milk Bread

Ingredients:

- 2 cups all-purpose flour
- 1/4 cup sugar
- 1/2 tsp salt
- 2 1/4 tsp active dry yeast
- 1/2 cup milk, warm
- 1/4 cup unsalted butter, melted
- 1 egg

Instructions:

1. In a small bowl, dissolve yeast and sugar in warm milk. Let sit for 5 minutes until foamy.
2. In a large bowl, combine flour and salt. Add the yeast mixture, melted butter, and egg.
3. Stir to form a dough and knead for 5-7 minutes until smooth.
4. Cover and let rise for 1 hour, or until doubled in size.
5. Preheat the oven to 375°F (190°C). Punch down the dough and shape it into a loaf.
6. Let it rise for another 30 minutes, then bake for 25-30 minutes until golden brown.

Cheese Stuffed Bread

Ingredients:

- 2 cups all-purpose flour
- 1 tbsp sugar
- 2 1/4 tsp active dry yeast
- 1 tsp salt
- 3/4 cup warm water
- 1 tbsp olive oil
- 1 cup shredded mozzarella cheese
- 1/2 cup grated Parmesan cheese

Instructions:

1. In a small bowl, dissolve sugar and yeast in warm water. Let sit for 5 minutes.
2. In a large bowl, combine flour and salt. Add the yeast mixture and olive oil. Stir to form a dough.
3. Knead the dough for 5-7 minutes, then let it rise for 1 hour.
4. Preheat the oven to 375°F (190°C). Punch down the dough and roll it out into a rectangle.
5. Sprinkle the cheese evenly over the dough, then roll it up tightly.
6. Place the roll in a greased loaf pan and let it rise for another 30 minutes.
7. Bake for 25-30 minutes, until golden brown and cheesy. Let cool slightly before slicing.

Olive Oil and Sea Salt Focaccia

Ingredients:

- 3 cups all-purpose flour
- 2 1/4 tsp active dry yeast
- 1 tbsp sugar
- 1 tsp salt
- 1 cup warm water
- 1/4 cup olive oil (plus extra for drizzling)
- Sea salt, for topping
- Fresh rosemary (optional)

Instructions:

1. In a small bowl, dissolve sugar and yeast in warm water. Let sit for 5 minutes.
2. In a large bowl, combine flour and salt. Add the yeast mixture and olive oil. Stir to form a dough.
3. Knead for 5-7 minutes, then cover and let rise for 1 hour.
4. Preheat the oven to 400°F (200°C). Punch down the dough and press it into a greased baking sheet.
5. Drizzle with olive oil and sprinkle with sea salt and rosemary.
6. Bake for 20-25 minutes, until golden brown.

Bacon Cheddar Bread

Ingredients:

- 2 cups all-purpose flour
- 1/4 cup sugar
- 1 tbsp baking powder
- 1/2 tsp salt
- 1 cup shredded cheddar cheese
- 1/2 cup cooked bacon, crumbled
- 1/2 cup milk
- 1/4 cup melted butter
- 1 egg

Instructions:

1. Preheat the oven to 375°F (190°C). Grease a 9x5-inch loaf pan.
2. In a large bowl, combine flour, sugar, baking powder, and salt. Add cheese and bacon.
3. In a separate bowl, whisk together milk, melted butter, and egg. Add to the dry ingredients.
4. Stir until combined, then pour the batter into the loaf pan.
5. Bake for 30-35 minutes, until golden brown. Let cool before slicing.

Sweet Potato Bread

Ingredients:

- 2 cups all-purpose flour
- 1 1/2 tsp baking soda
- 1 tsp cinnamon
- 1/2 tsp nutmeg
- 1/2 tsp salt
- 1/2 cup brown sugar
- 1/4 cup white sugar
- 1/2 cup vegetable oil
- 2 large eggs
- 1 cup mashed sweet potato (cooked)
- 1 tsp vanilla extract
- 1/2 cup chopped walnuts (optional)

Instructions:

1. Preheat the oven to 350°F (175°C). Grease a 9x5-inch loaf pan.
2. In a medium bowl, whisk together flour, baking soda, cinnamon, nutmeg, and salt.
3. In a large bowl, mix the sugars, oil, eggs, sweet potato, and vanilla until smooth.
4. Gradually add the dry ingredients to the wet mixture, stirring until just combined. Fold in walnuts, if using.
5. Pour the batter into the prepared pan and smooth the top.
6. Bake for 60-70 minutes, or until a toothpick comes out clean. Let cool before slicing.

Apple and Walnut Bread

Ingredients:

- 2 cups all-purpose flour
- 1 tsp cinnamon
- 1/2 tsp baking soda
- 1/2 tsp salt
- 1/2 cup sugar
- 1/4 cup brown sugar
- 2 large eggs
- 1/2 cup vegetable oil
- 1 cup peeled, grated apple
- 1/2 cup chopped walnuts
- 1 tsp vanilla extract

Instructions:

1. Preheat the oven to 350°F (175°C). Grease a 9x5-inch loaf pan.
2. In a bowl, mix the flour, cinnamon, baking soda, and salt.
3. In a separate bowl, whisk the sugar, brown sugar, eggs, oil, and vanilla until smooth.
4. Add the grated apple to the wet ingredients, then fold in the dry ingredients until just combined.
5. Gently fold in the walnuts.
6. Pour the batter into the prepared pan and bake for 50-60 minutes, or until golden and a toothpick comes out clean. Let cool before slicing.

Hot Cross Buns

Ingredients:

- 4 cups all-purpose flour
- 1/2 cup sugar
- 1 tbsp active dry yeast
- 1/2 tsp salt
- 1 1/2 tsp ground cinnamon
- 1/2 tsp ground nutmeg
- 1/2 cup milk
- 1/4 cup water
- 1/4 cup butter
- 2 large eggs
- 1/2 cup currants or raisins
- 1 tbsp milk (for glazing)
- Icing (for cross)

Instructions:

1. In a small saucepan, heat the milk, water, and butter until warm. Remove from heat and let cool slightly.
2. In a large bowl, combine the flour, sugar, yeast, salt, cinnamon, and nutmeg.
3. Add the warm milk mixture, eggs, and currants to the dry ingredients. Stir to form a dough.
4. Knead the dough for 10 minutes until smooth. Let rise for 1 hour, or until doubled in size.
5. Preheat the oven to 375°F (190°C). Punch down the dough and divide into 12 portions. Shape into buns and place on a greased baking sheet.
6. Let the buns rise for another 30 minutes. Brush with 1 tbsp milk.
7. Bake for 18-20 minutes, until golden brown. Drizzle with icing in a cross shape before serving.

Stuffed Garlic Bread

Ingredients:

- 2 cups all-purpose flour
- 2 1/4 tsp active dry yeast
- 1 tbsp sugar
- 1 tsp salt
- 3/4 cup warm water
- 3 tbsp olive oil
- 4 cloves garlic, minced
- 1/2 cup melted butter
- 1/2 cup grated mozzarella cheese

Instructions:

1. In a bowl, dissolve sugar and yeast in warm water. Let sit for 5 minutes until foamy.
2. In a large bowl, combine flour and salt. Add the yeast mixture and olive oil, stirring to form a dough.
3. Knead the dough for 5-7 minutes, then cover and let rise for 1 hour.
4. Preheat the oven to 375°F (190°C). Punch down the dough and roll it out into a rectangle.
5. Mix garlic with melted butter and brush over the dough. Sprinkle mozzarella evenly on top.
6. Roll the dough into a log and place it in a greased baking pan. Let it rise for another 30 minutes.
7. Bake for 20-25 minutes, or until golden brown. Serve warm.

Tomato Basil Bread

Ingredients:

- 2 cups all-purpose flour
- 1/4 cup sun-dried tomatoes, chopped
- 1/4 cup fresh basil, chopped
- 1 tbsp olive oil
- 1/2 tsp salt
- 1 tsp sugar
- 2 1/4 tsp active dry yeast
- 1 cup warm water
- 1/2 tsp garlic powder (optional)

Instructions:

1. Dissolve the sugar and yeast in warm water and let sit for 5 minutes until foamy.
2. In a large bowl, combine flour, salt, and garlic powder (if using).
3. Add the yeast mixture, olive oil, sun-dried tomatoes, and basil. Stir to form a dough.
4. Knead the dough for 5-7 minutes, then cover and let rise for 1 hour.
5. Preheat the oven to 375°F (190°C). Punch down the dough and shape it into a loaf.
6. Let the dough rise for another 30 minutes. Bake for 30-35 minutes until golden brown.

Blueberry Lemon Bread

Ingredients:

- 2 cups all-purpose flour
- 1 tsp baking powder
- 1/2 tsp salt
- 1/2 cup sugar
- 1/4 cup butter, softened
- 2 large eggs
- 1/2 cup milk
- Zest of 1 lemon
- 1 1/2 cups fresh blueberries

Instructions:

1. Preheat the oven to 350°F (175°C). Grease a 9x5-inch loaf pan.
2. In a small bowl, whisk together flour, baking powder, and salt.
3. In a large bowl, beat together sugar, butter, and eggs until smooth. Add the milk and lemon zest.
4. Gradually add the dry ingredients to the wet ingredients, mixing until just combined.
5. Gently fold in the blueberries.
6. Pour the batter into the prepared pan and bake for 50-60 minutes, or until a toothpick comes out clean.

Spicy Cheddar Cornbread

Ingredients:

- 1 1/2 cups cornmeal
- 1 cup all-purpose flour
- 1 tbsp sugar
- 1 tsp baking powder
- 1/2 tsp baking soda
- 1/2 tsp salt
- 1 cup shredded sharp cheddar cheese
- 1/4 cup jalapeño peppers, diced
- 1 cup buttermilk
- 1/4 cup vegetable oil
- 2 large eggs

Instructions:

1. Preheat the oven to 375°F (190°C). Grease a 9x9-inch baking dish.
2. In a large bowl, combine cornmeal, flour, sugar, baking powder, baking soda, and salt.
3. Add the cheese and jalapeños, stirring to distribute evenly.
4. In a separate bowl, whisk together buttermilk, oil, and eggs.
5. Add the wet ingredients to the dry ingredients and stir until just combined.
6. Pour the batter into the prepared dish and bake for 20-25 minutes, or until golden brown.

Chocolate Chip Banana Bread

Ingredients:

- 2 ripe bananas, mashed
- 1 cup sugar
- 1/2 cup melted butter
- 2 large eggs
- 1 1/2 cups all-purpose flour
- 1 tsp baking soda
- 1/4 tsp salt
- 1/2 cup chocolate chips

Instructions:

1. Preheat the oven to 350°F (175°C). Grease a 9x5-inch loaf pan.
2. In a bowl, mash the bananas and mix with sugar and melted butter.
3. Add eggs and stir to combine. In a separate bowl, whisk together flour, baking soda, and salt.
4. Gradually add the dry ingredients to the wet mixture, stirring until just combined.
5. Fold in the chocolate chips.
6. Pour the batter into the prepared pan and bake for 60-70 minutes, or until a toothpick comes out clean.

Cinnamon Rolls

Ingredients:

- 3 cups all-purpose flour
- 1/4 cup sugar
- 2 1/4 tsp active dry yeast
- 1/2 tsp salt
- 1 cup warm milk
- 1/4 cup melted butter
- 1 large egg
- 1/2 cup brown sugar
- 2 tbsp ground cinnamon
- 1/4 cup unsalted butter, softened
- 1 cup powdered sugar (for icing)
- 1 tbsp milk (for icing)

Instructions:

1. In a small bowl, dissolve sugar and yeast in warm milk. Let sit for 5 minutes.
2. In a large bowl, combine flour and salt. Add the yeast mixture, melted butter, and egg. Stir until a dough forms.
3. Knead the dough for 5-7 minutes, then cover and let rise for 1 hour.
4. Preheat the oven to 350°F (175°C). Punch down the dough and roll it out into a rectangle.
5. Spread softened butter over the dough, then sprinkle with brown sugar and cinnamon.
6. Roll the dough into a log and slice into 12 rolls. Place them in a greased baking dish.
7. Let the rolls rise for 30 minutes, then bake for 20-25 minutes.
8. In a small bowl, mix powdered sugar with milk to make icing, and drizzle over the warm rolls.

Peach and Almond Bread

Ingredients:

- 2 cups all-purpose flour
- 1 tsp baking powder
- 1/2 tsp baking soda
- 1/2 tsp salt
- 1 tsp ground cinnamon
- 1/2 cup sugar
- 1/4 cup brown sugar
- 1/2 cup vegetable oil
- 2 large eggs
- 1 tsp vanilla extract
- 1 cup diced fresh peaches
- 1/2 cup sliced almonds

Instructions:

1. Preheat the oven to 350°F (175°C). Grease a 9x5-inch loaf pan.
2. In a medium bowl, whisk together the flour, baking powder, baking soda, salt, and cinnamon.
3. In a large bowl, mix together the sugars, oil, eggs, and vanilla until smooth.
4. Gradually add the dry ingredients to the wet ingredients, stirring until just combined.
5. Fold in the diced peaches and almonds.
6. Pour the batter into the prepared loaf pan and smooth the top.
7. Bake for 60-70 minutes, or until a toothpick comes out clean. Let cool before slicing.

Pecan Bread

Ingredients:

- 2 cups all-purpose flour
- 1 cup brown sugar
- 1/2 tsp salt
- 1 tsp baking soda
- 1 tsp ground cinnamon
- 1/2 cup unsalted butter, softened
- 2 large eggs
- 1 cup buttermilk
- 1 tsp vanilla extract
- 1 cup chopped pecans

Instructions:

1. Preheat the oven to 350°F (175°C). Grease a 9x5-inch loaf pan.
2. In a medium bowl, whisk together the flour, brown sugar, salt, baking soda, and cinnamon.
3. In a large bowl, beat together the butter, eggs, buttermilk, and vanilla until smooth.
4. Gradually add the dry ingredients to the wet mixture, stirring until just combined.
5. Fold in the chopped pecans.
6. Pour the batter into the prepared pan and smooth the top.
7. Bake for 60-70 minutes, or until golden brown and a toothpick comes out clean.

Cranberry Almond Bread

Ingredients:

- 2 cups all-purpose flour
- 1 tsp baking powder
- 1/2 tsp baking soda
- 1/2 tsp salt
- 1/2 cup sugar
- 1/2 cup orange juice
- 1/4 cup vegetable oil
- 2 large eggs
- 1 tsp vanilla extract
- 1 cup dried cranberries
- 1/2 cup sliced almonds

Instructions:

1. Preheat the oven to 350°F (175°C). Grease a 9x5-inch loaf pan.
2. In a medium bowl, whisk together the flour, baking powder, baking soda, salt, and sugar.
3. In a large bowl, whisk together the orange juice, oil, eggs, and vanilla.
4. Gradually add the dry ingredients to the wet mixture, stirring until just combined.
5. Gently fold in the cranberries and almonds.
6. Pour the batter into the prepared loaf pan and smooth the top.
7. Bake for 60-70 minutes, or until golden and a toothpick comes out clean. Let cool before slicing.

Herb and Parmesan Breadsticks

Ingredients:

- 1 1/2 cups all-purpose flour
- 1/2 tsp salt
- 1 tbsp sugar
- 1 tsp instant yeast
- 1/2 cup warm water
- 1/4 cup olive oil
- 1/4 cup grated Parmesan cheese
- 1 tsp dried Italian herbs (such as basil, oregano, thyme)
- 1/2 tsp garlic powder

Instructions:

1. Preheat the oven to 400°F (200°C). Line a baking sheet with parchment paper.
2. In a small bowl, dissolve the sugar and yeast in warm water. Let sit for 5 minutes until foamy.
3. In a large bowl, combine the flour and salt. Add the yeast mixture and olive oil. Stir to form a dough.
4. Knead the dough for 5-7 minutes, then cover and let rise for 1 hour.
5. Punch down the dough and divide it into small pieces. Roll each piece into a stick shape.
6. Place the breadsticks on the prepared baking sheet, sprinkle with Parmesan cheese, Italian herbs, and garlic powder.
7. Bake for 12-15 minutes, or until golden brown. Serve warm.

Asiago Cheese Bread

Ingredients:

- 2 cups all-purpose flour
- 1 1/2 tsp salt
- 1 tbsp sugar
- 2 tsp active dry yeast
- 1 cup warm water
- 2 tbsp olive oil
- 1 cup shredded Asiago cheese
- 1/2 tsp garlic powder (optional)

Instructions:

1. Preheat the oven to 375°F (190°C). Grease a 9x5-inch loaf pan.
2. In a small bowl, dissolve sugar and yeast in warm water. Let sit for 5 minutes until foamy.
3. In a large bowl, combine the flour and salt. Add the yeast mixture and olive oil, stirring to form a dough.
4. Knead the dough for 5-7 minutes, then cover and let rise for 1 hour.
5. Gently fold in the Asiago cheese and garlic powder (if using).
6. Pour the dough into the prepared pan and bake for 30-35 minutes, or until golden brown and a toothpick comes out clean.

Pretzel Bread

Ingredients:

- 3 cups all-purpose flour
- 1 tsp salt
- 1 tbsp sugar
- 2 1/4 tsp active dry yeast
- 1 cup warm water
- 1/4 cup baking soda
- 1 egg, beaten
- Coarse salt for topping

Instructions:

1. Preheat the oven to 400°F (200°C). Line a baking sheet with parchment paper.
2. In a small bowl, dissolve sugar and yeast in warm water. Let sit for 5 minutes until foamy.
3. In a large bowl, combine the flour and salt. Add the yeast mixture and stir to form a dough.
4. Knead the dough for 5-7 minutes, then cover and let rise for 1 hour.
5. Punch down the dough and divide it into 8 equal portions. Roll each portion into a ball or log shape.
6. Bring a pot of water to a boil, and add the baking soda. Carefully drop each dough ball into the water for 30 seconds.
7. Place the boiled dough on the baking sheet, brush with beaten egg, and sprinkle with coarse salt.
8. Bake for 15-20 minutes, or until golden brown.

Coconut Bread

Ingredients:

- 2 cups all-purpose flour
- 1/2 cup shredded coconut
- 1 tsp baking powder
- 1/2 tsp salt
- 1/2 cup sugar
- 2 large eggs
- 1/2 cup coconut milk
- 1/4 cup vegetable oil
- 1 tsp vanilla extract

Instructions:

1. Preheat the oven to 350°F (175°C). Grease a 9x5-inch loaf pan.
2. In a medium bowl, whisk together the flour, shredded coconut, baking powder, and salt.
3. In a separate bowl, whisk together the sugar, eggs, coconut milk, oil, and vanilla extract.
4. Gradually add the wet ingredients to the dry ingredients, stirring until just combined.
5. Pour the batter into the prepared pan and smooth the top.
6. Bake for 55-60 minutes, or until golden and a toothpick comes out clean. Let cool before slicing.

Maple Pecan Bread

Ingredients:

- 2 cups all-purpose flour
- 1 tsp baking powder
- 1/2 tsp baking soda
- 1/2 tsp salt
- 1/2 cup maple syrup
- 1/4 cup brown sugar
- 1/2 cup unsalted butter, softened
- 2 large eggs
- 1/2 cup milk
- 1 tsp vanilla extract
- 1 cup chopped pecans

Instructions:

1. Preheat the oven to 350°F (175°C). Grease a 9x5-inch loaf pan.
2. In a medium bowl, whisk together the flour, baking powder, baking soda, and salt.
3. In a large bowl, beat together the maple syrup, brown sugar, butter, eggs, milk, and vanilla until smooth.
4. Gradually add the dry ingredients to the wet ingredients, mixing until just combined.
5. Fold in the chopped pecans.
6. Pour the batter into the prepared pan and smooth the top.
7. Bake for 60-70 minutes, or until a toothpick inserted into the center comes out clean. Let cool before slicing.

Lemon Poppy Seed Bread

Ingredients:

- 2 cups all-purpose flour
- 1 tsp baking powder
- 1/2 tsp baking soda
- 1/2 tsp salt
- 1/2 cup sugar
- 1/2 cup unsalted butter, softened
- 2 large eggs
- 1/2 cup sour cream
- 1/4 cup milk
- Zest of 1 lemon
- 2 tbsp lemon juice
- 1 tbsp poppy seeds

Instructions:

1. Preheat the oven to 350°F (175°C). Grease a 9x5-inch loaf pan.
2. In a medium bowl, whisk together the flour, baking powder, baking soda, and salt.
3. In a large bowl, beat together the sugar, butter, eggs, sour cream, milk, lemon zest, and lemon juice until smooth.
4. Gradually add the dry ingredients to the wet ingredients, mixing until just combined.
5. Stir in the poppy seeds.
6. Pour the batter into the prepared pan and smooth the top.
7. Bake for 50-60 minutes, or until golden and a toothpick comes out clean. Let cool before slicing.

Fig and Walnut Bread

Ingredients:

- 2 cups all-purpose flour
- 1/2 tsp baking soda
- 1/2 tsp salt
- 1 tsp ground cinnamon
- 1/2 cup brown sugar
- 2 large eggs
- 1/2 cup vegetable oil
- 1/2 cup sour cream
- 1 tsp vanilla extract
- 1/2 cup chopped figs
- 1/2 cup chopped walnuts

Instructions:

1. Preheat the oven to 350°F (175°C). Grease a 9x5-inch loaf pan.
2. In a medium bowl, whisk together the flour, baking soda, salt, and cinnamon.
3. In a large bowl, beat together the brown sugar, eggs, oil, sour cream, and vanilla extract until smooth.
4. Gradually add the dry ingredients to the wet mixture, stirring until just combined.
5. Fold in the chopped figs and walnuts.
6. Pour the batter into the prepared pan and smooth the top.
7. Bake for 55-65 minutes, or until golden brown and a toothpick comes out clean. Let cool before slicing.

Sweet Cornbread with Jalapeños

Ingredients:

- 1 1/2 cups cornmeal
- 1 cup all-purpose flour
- 1/4 cup sugar
- 1 tbsp baking powder
- 1/2 tsp salt
- 1 cup buttermilk
- 1/4 cup unsalted butter, melted
- 2 large eggs
- 2-3 jalapeños, finely chopped
- 1/2 cup corn kernels (optional)

Instructions:

1. Preheat the oven to 400°F (200°C). Grease an 8x8-inch baking dish.
2. In a large bowl, combine the cornmeal, flour, sugar, baking powder, and salt.
3. In a separate bowl, whisk together the buttermilk, melted butter, and eggs until smooth.
4. Gradually add the wet ingredients to the dry ingredients, stirring until just combined.
5. Fold in the chopped jalapeños and corn kernels (if using).
6. Pour the batter into the prepared dish and smooth the top.
7. Bake for 20-25 minutes, or until golden brown and a toothpick comes out clean. Let cool slightly before serving.

Carrot Raisin Bread

Ingredients:

- 2 cups all-purpose flour
- 1 tsp baking soda
- 1/2 tsp salt
- 1 tsp ground cinnamon
- 1/2 cup sugar
- 1/2 cup brown sugar
- 1/2 cup vegetable oil
- 3 large eggs
- 2 cups grated carrots
- 1/2 cup raisins
- 1 tsp vanilla extract

Instructions:

1. Preheat the oven to 350°F (175°C). Grease a 9x5-inch loaf pan.
2. In a medium bowl, whisk together the flour, baking soda, salt, and cinnamon.
3. In a large bowl, beat together the sugars, oil, eggs, grated carrots, raisins, and vanilla extract until smooth.
4. Gradually add the dry ingredients to the wet mixture, stirring until just combined.
5. Pour the batter into the prepared pan and smooth the top.
6. Bake for 55-65 minutes, or until golden brown and a toothpick comes out clean. Let cool before slicing.

Bacon and Chive Bread

Ingredients:

- 2 cups all-purpose flour
- 1 tbsp baking powder
- 1/2 tsp salt
- 1/2 cup cooked bacon, chopped
- 1/4 cup chopped fresh chives
- 1/2 cup shredded cheddar cheese
- 2 large eggs
- 1/2 cup milk
- 1/4 cup unsalted butter, melted

Instructions:

1. Preheat the oven to 350°F (175°C). Grease a 9x5-inch loaf pan.
2. In a medium bowl, whisk together the flour, baking powder, and salt.
3. In a separate bowl, beat together the eggs, milk, and melted butter until smooth.
4. Gradually add the dry ingredients to the wet mixture, stirring until just combined.
5. Fold in the chopped bacon, chives, and shredded cheddar cheese.
6. Pour the batter into the prepared pan and smooth the top.
7. Bake for 45-55 minutes, or until golden and a toothpick comes out clean. Let cool before slicing.